THIRD WINTER
IN OUR SECOND COUNTRY

Third Winter
in Our Second Country

poems by Andres Rojas

Rojas, Andres
1st edition

ISBN: 978-1-949487-05-3
Library of Congress Control Number: 2021930891

Interior design by Matt Mauch
Cover art by
Cover design by Joel Coggins
Editing by Tayve Neese, Sarah Dumitrascu

Trio House Press, Inc.
Ponte Vedra Beach, FL

To contact the author, send an email to tayveneese@gmail.com.

For my poetry teachers: Marilyn DeSimone,
Kevin Bezner, Joan New, Debora Greger,
William Logan, Michael Hofmann,
and Donald Justice.

And for my wife Melinda, always.

Table of Contents

I

New Year's Eve

December shuts its door on night's high wall,
eye-clear sky this morning, gusts rattling cages

of brambles now, a field's yield of warblers
dropped starving from the clouds. Our town goes on

with its drizzle and leashed dogs. We pass ghosts
lean as winter weeds or cattle wire: they know

what they are and keep their distance like fog. Again
we turn our faces to lessen the wind's sting. Again

we hope to be neither prey nor hunger,
the children in them nor the chain-link kennels.

Confession

Time is on the prowl
and the universe is nowhere near

sated: black hole, meteor, storm surge.
The bones of life splinter

and choke us. My grandparents
fed an orphan, who orphaned them

and me, his son—I, too, left them
at their door after forgetting

our last hug. A revolution
drowned them: I let myself believe

when you are going under
you swim first for yourself.

I was heating Campbell's in a can
and counting Marlboros

when ripples of their deaths
found me. They'd each

been dead for months.
I cried, yes, until I didn't.

And then I didn't.

Watercolors at Year's End

Your pines were, rightly, secondary,
a wash of sun and sky, branches

thick as velvet pillows, clumsy
as my questions: How do clouds darken

to nightmare? Are dreams smoke-blue?
What color, love? Yours were non-answers

I translated, broken strokes, a trembling
brush you barely held, subjects muddled

as your verbs—the cramped thumbs
of apple boughs, a flight of birds

rising, darkness rising its slow wings,
your eyes two iceberg tips

sharp as broken window glass,
red as your hands, distant

as cedars lapped by heavy mist.
What depths you knew

kept your hulk intact,
palms and fingers bandaged,

then scarred but free again
to try your bidding.

Like your room, what was inside
is what was lost: gone,

the woman bundled in bed,
tossed like a passenger at sea,

the bottles empty of their pills,
water cold in a cold cup,

the body at last empty and at rest.
Am I to answer now? You are beyond

my every skill. Your city under snow
is salt and sand, your days gray

with overcast and drizzle,
yourself gray and pencil-drawn,

unseen, in any case, but for what
pigments hide you, blue stars

weightless on your lids. What color,
love? It is a shadow, a stain

that spreads like failure or remorse,
never again the child's easy palette,

never the grace of a blank page.

Blucher, Arendt, A Wildland Fire

Turn off the TV, light of the World
Series, light of Dawn Ultra, light

anything, the cherub moon
on a ceiling of stars,

Newton's candle,
New Mexico's *stella nova*.

Turn off your Black Irish skin
in cotton, your hair's charged cloud

on borrowed sheets,
the brown girl

still in brown sand, the signs
of people on goat trails,

refugee and migrant.
Above us, satellites fall

too fast to fall, godlike
over desert bones

turning dust devils,
the half-life of grit

we drive through,
so many lines on a map:

how they gleam,
our metal animals,

their traces invisible
as breathing.

In a dim taqueria,
a waitress still wading

into English
clears our mess.

All we've seen
others have before.

It's night. The moon
slips further away

from us
like our lives.

The Dental Assistant in the V-J Day Photo

is twenty-one, in a foreign port. The Holocaust
fogged her parents out. Maybe in cages.
Maybe underground. The war is over.

Millions not even a thought, but the war is over.
A body, a country, time: these are the cages
she reels from, the blasts of other holocausts.

Trail Mountain
from the Cherokee

What is left of crags
is as much riven inheritance

as the rough-winged swallows
buzzing the rhododendrons,

hunters on the fly as are we all,
each laurel an *axis mundi*

no more native than the clouds
invisible today: what is gone

could last through anything,
except what came. That isn't right.

What remains is what remains
always, for a certain time: water

drawn four thousand feet
downhill, a wafting keen,

dusk clear as any conscience
that does not look too far afield—

next ridgeline, state line,
halfway across to the Pacific.

St. Augustine in Ariel's Island

He plagiarized a hull, unmoored his eyes
at the dock, tried to read what faith

had nail-scratched on bulkheads.
Taught us coins and boots, six

Hebrew words for lion (*kefir, lavi,
layish, shahal, shahatz,* also

the one that, starving in its den,
watches the soul). And, unoriginally,

sin. Knew nothing eternal
but had words for it,

his Lord a book having no body
but legions of mouths. Told us

the spirit is a ship at sail
invisible in fog, the flesh

a skiff's trace lost to waves. Told us
the storm was near, but that we

had been made ready: shoes
off, pockets emptied, our eyes shut.

Kahina

Manat
In'am Sabahan

Almost still a boy. Stalky.
As a reed. A rod.
Your words on my ear,
the desert in your voice.

Even here, water murmurs
like your uncle's caravan.
Like years, certain aches.
Like the life

of the starved stray
on your black dog's fangs,
snarls dark as winter-crop
thunder clouds.

Like questions: the sieve
of a body dying, blood
on my bloody arms,
eyes on mine

anything but quiet.
You chided, *Such a girl*
to let her hands
into the mouths of curs.

Uzza
Salaam Alay-kum

The only haven
where I belong:
what you revealed.

For it, any wilderness,
the recitations of armor

on the day of battle.

My heart is a box
full of swords: pray
you do not open it.

Or pry it so.
Whom a blade may slay
it may also deliver.

Allat
Walay-kum Salaam

You were horizon
to my wandering,

grackle to my earth-
shadow, your call

a foot trail sudden out of brush,
a spring amid deaf sand.

Now you are my plectrum,
I your plucked string.

Thus I will sing mercy,
even if not yours: fever

I know, and noon heat.
And the break of fever,

cool sleep that sates.
The bite of thorns.

The body's self-love
bent on healing. Not why

but that otherwise
is silence. Of this I sing:

you the flesh and I the callus.
I the feet and you the road.

The Prodigal's Next Life

He forgave first
not forgiving
himself before

as he forgave
the dust trailing his steps
faithful as his shadow,

as one who has gotten
away with something
forgives a fallen nestling,

a lost yearling,
another self
who never turned back

from a land
of lean cattle
and empty of bees.

Jesus Drowns in the Sea of Galilee
...and I will make you fishers of men

Sometimes

life is more
than.

Sometimes
life is more.

Then

for years
(years)

we lay
children

side by side
like carp,

grind them fine
into our fingertips:

scale-powder,
bone meal,

isinglass.

Others
we sprinkle

with natron or sea
salt, with words

to save the lost

or, maybe,
preserve them.

Virgilian Fortunes
from the Aeneid

Weeping I left my native coast,
my harbor, the skull-bare plain
where once stood Troy.

Deep into exile I was thrust, I,
my companions, my wife,
our household gods, the gods

of all our people, destiny's refuse,
flotsam all in waves we sowed
with friends. And every day

was hardship at our elbow,
each narrow ship an agony,
each groan of wind and rigging

a new curse, until at last
we threw our bodies to dry earth.
The only crop we had that year was death.

I Am Prometheus
after J. T. Burke

At my chalice-smooth fingers
bronzed as judgment trumpets, one hand
glacier-blue, the other lilies and teeth—

at my terebinth ribs, my camel-thorn breasts
thick with phoenix-egg pearls, rich
as the stories you tell your own import—

at my columbine liver and womb,
        the daily hummingbird feeds:

you could exhaust your life
        and miss it,

this sky nothing like a grave
in its illusion of infinity, my wings
cruciform under a crown's fixed diamonds,

the sun's stolen seeds, a hearth's
peacock flames, until your city
lies stripped to marrow and ash.

Here boys played at rocks.
Here virgins were trussed:

I am not the body
nailed to this volcano.

I am the volcano
holding her breath.

Soon Before All Light Is Gone

Frame *now* as a hand like a wave
on night's sea, crashing. Still

a child, he peels seconds
off the evening

like insect wings:
boots multiply, breed

mud, see there's no getting
out.

       In the movie-set
courtroom, smoke

refracts shadows
and meat-marbled

light:
       the war criminal

shrugs in his death
shackles, bored of resignation,

pointing fingers harden
to bullets and skulls. Now

frame the boy as he fears
for the sun's canary egg

as it breaks to be healed. And frame
how he cries for dead cicadas

oblivious
to the will of the swarm.

December Doe

High Springs, Florida
for/after Eduardo C. Corral

Every miracle is an escape:

windshield ice, her hulk
closer than my headlights,

a second hand crossing midnight,
a sleight of fate or faith.

Later, I walk the grass
in a Greek chorus of frost,

a *Kyrie eleison* this side

of her leap, the road stitched in time
between us: a fleeting scatter of does

three weeks back, near here,
a scramble of white sails—

those of galleons or rafts—
toward a horizon of forest.

October

for/after Laura Pollán

The streets of this city are laid on teeth. [*bones & trash*]
You have to dig to see them. They wear out
the human in your hands. You serve your nights

in dreams of fingers clawing, skeletal,
at rocks hard as the ironshore's canines.

At the old Hilton lounge, the name now ash,
foreign reporters don't bother with such.
Stories. They want stories. So they wait.

So men on hunger strike fade more each day.
So women march with locked arms. So they wield

sword-flowers, scabbed-over wounds, white banners,
their torches shedding sparks that die on stones
smooth as toothless gums, too ill and too young.

The police batter in and crush more than bone.
The sun bleeds, then it's gone. Night grins with stars.

Swan Song

I, in time, am sick of living
with myself, anytime soon

as alibi, rose of Jericho's
odd duckling bloom,

coal a thorn on the lungs
playing its long game. And you,

a miner's daughter
in hate with her last decade,

hands up like a policeman's
bullet's corpse: dark

with no chance of humor.
What is left for transformation?

This beach we walk? Its few
bittersweet clams and baby's ears,

terse diamonds on the littoral's midden?
Tomorrow, this same time of day

will pass you by in another continent,
but for now, you toe-dig at a stone

crab's shell. *Molted or dead?*
Some have looked on their children

like this. Or nieces or brothers.
The Atlantic breathes less each year,

and the tides rustle fewer coquinas,
but the answer is *molted.*

Third Winter in Our Second Country
for/after Charles Simic

On this crystal-fanged night
      the unflinching stars

are an old family
      photo:

so many here
      gone already.

In the Dark Times

I fix a coat from air to clothe my fears,
accept tomorrow will be full of cracks
and their attendant gusts: the roof
over my life may be past repair.
       I wait for words

sent out like crows to return, even
if soaked, wings like broken branches.
Buy a stranger a burger. Hand another
paper money. Know they'll both stomach
       hunger anew.

I drop each of my hours like a crumb.
I won't walk this way again. My days
line up like inmates and clap hands.
They clap hands for me,
       and I sing.

II

From the Lost Letters to Matias Perez, Aeronaut

I remember what you saw—a boulevard
of moonlight on water, waves

like names on a chart,
your absence, like weather, a given.

My father disappeared
into another country

when I was five—why
not you, a hundred years before?

My first memory is him.
He carries me against his neck,

the beach receding as he walks us
into a life I don't yet see.

Sometimes I wish
that were the last of him

I kept. Of what's beyond us,
we know nothing, or we know

enough, the particulars of loss:
sand, the westering sun,

a wind-seized balloon,
the sea.

What Vallejo Calls Notre Dame Bridge

will not let him cross in peace,
its black stones breaking to white chatter
like parrots, the smell of eucalyptus

clamoring in the autumn rain
as if it were the tropics, Lima,
fifteen years before, as if Vallejo

were not already Vallejo:
lush bronze greenery
on the cathedral, the market alive

with oranges, sunflower hearts,
sweet potatoes priced for haggling,
Paris still a budding orchid,

the prize of a florist's stand, white
as the Madonna's marble throat, moist
as a sponge dipped in vinegar.

...mmertime
Jacksonville, Florida

I tell her I've seen a hawk
beak a pigeon cold
on a branch by the Wells Fargo,
a bile she-cat
take a squirrel in Hemming Plaza.

Older

than us, I tell her,
hunger is patient
as the river's belt-narrow bend,
the dogwood stone
smooth as an ax handle

for the lean Confederate dead.
And it's all a long weeding,
I tell her. She doesn't answer,
eyes blue as blue shadows,
sharp as the manicured grass

we hunt

for my gold ring, a fight
over money, what else,
her purse-flashlight bright
only in night so dark,
so dim it seems distant, a promise,

light waiting for itself.
I tell her its beam shines
like milk after hard fast,
a debt forgiven, if unpaid.
Shut up, she says, *and keep*

looking.

And it's all a long weeding,

I say, the only answer
a snap of flag on air
on July-fire male voice
from the angled

façade

of Plaza Jewelers.
I've been drinking razor soup,
it says to two men wearing
bedrolls like life preservers.
We're going down, one says,

to the Kings Street shelter.
And I feel above us its specter,
eagle talons chill, feathers
like eyeteeth, horned head
sneering. It will pick them clean,

our bones.

I see its shadow fall slant
on your nose, itself
slant on your small skull,
so beautiful, so much blood
keeping our skulls beautiful.

I hate I get like this.
I hate you can see it.
When life tells you something,
I say, believe it.
I do, you say, and *keep*

looking.

Flying Wallendas

Some say *tightrope*
though it sags in the middle
until you step in
and the slack centers
on you. Others,
highwire, a pencil-
thin contrail
two flag poles

above concrete—
drop a mannequin
and consider ribcage
and lungs. I say
skywalking, and no net
can ease that plummet—
sky-walk,
sky-fall.

Retrace with me
that line we saw
only later,
a black thread
on night's tarp,
our pause at the step-
board altar,
two bodies leaning

into future space
daring luck
to waver, the wire
invisible below—
until death do its part—
each syllable of sole
on metal a vow:
Steady. Steady on.

Dead People's Things for Sale

Here lies a fragment of their affection,
two clay-olive bronze chairs
across a shield-round table,
a planter in its middle for green shoots.

On it they shared figs from a tree
in their rental garden, held each like a toad's
pale belly sliced to marigolds
or to a knee's meager pomegranate flesh.

I was there. I remember.
The tree is gone. So is the garden,
the block plowed flat for a hospital's garage.
The table we saved for a later rending.

Learning to See in Another Language

Because the snapper
before us don't have their eyes
open, nor the candles

that were bees' bellies
or whatever, and no
plate is a landmine, even

metaphorically, and I know
what counts is not *what*
but *where*, right, and we

agree resurrection is a myth
and thus not false,
and hellfire, also myth

and not untrue. *And how
can you eat, how can you eat,*
says just too loud

a man at another table,
*knowing we know
people on the kill*

list? But that doesn't
really happen, does it,
as the interpreter tells us

after we finish: *That was not
what you saw. That
was not what you saw at all.*

Mayport Ospreys

Wild things are made from human histories.
— Helen Macdonald

The last boats brought back the tide
in their holds, twilight-rust
on fittings resigned to old age. There,
the sun's jaundiced heel. Not yet
the bare-kneecap moon among clouds.

Earlier, the overcast flew its rags
              and vernal floods around
vestal dunes. Willets
tip-toed each wave's last slow spill,
the ocean's grab sharp as cold talons.

An osprey, prow-like, cuts
seaward to the coming gloom, easy
past us whom it need not flee nor stalk.
What other storms don't trouble
its mind? That it kills? That no wing

shelters it from chance? You'd think
              it'd covet
the habitual plovers and turnstones,
or from a seagreen nimbus
ambush seagulls. But like the boats

and us, it holds to its tack
as a matter of course,
and its craving is fish: blind
beyond their element, harried,
dead to what shadows lurk above.

Using the Scout's Handbook While Learning English

Not yet a full animal, no longer
fully cub, sunlight green on me
through summer's high canopy, a stream
mud-cheeked from last night's rains:
from fifteen years on, I see
myself, lean for my age, light-boned
as a hawk, fleeing a housing project
not so much life-preserver
as a hurricane's next island. But today,
the tallest I've been and growing,
I think I've come for animals.
          From their world, mine
must seem both comically unstealthy
and full of sudden excitements. But I
see, as I still see, both the signs on the mud
and the need to read them, their tracks
a test for the Handbook.
And it serves: a pair of racoons, deer,
and, later, what I wanted to be bear
but was just a dog, the known names
besides the mysteries:
muskrat, grouse, skunk. And I
don't yet know it, but I'll remember
this day, when I asked and was answered,
when the world spoke its persistent language
and I, with due care, understood.

Out of Cuba

Taking *from*
to mean *taken from*.

To no longer have
as mother's milk.

To have no more
to lose: baby

teeth. Meaning
which of my cells

now alive
were alive then.

We Argued in Spanish Before We Argued in English

Proud of my first
I showed it to her

Hurt like an alien
ripping out of my deltoid

And I had not to cry
nine hours it took

A life-like heart
wrapped in barbed wire

Madre above
Hittite cuneiform below

A language with a script
borrowed from another

As far back as I
could reach a mother tongue

Modir Matar
Mayr in Armenian

Almost Mary
now and in the hour

She cried said everyone
would make me for a thug

Called that night
I said *If I could*

I can't but if I could
I'd choose you again.

Rifle Grease, Gunpowder, Dead Fish
Escambray

So the newspapers let go
like oysters, the radio waves
lobster-boiled in the censored air: we
tucked our weapons

from the seafood warehouse,
climbed heavy at the gunnels
to the rising mountains.

(A barrel's flowers:
red scallop over the left nipple,
red scallop on the right,
burst of paella from the belly.)

We bathed fording a stream
or in rain. Our skins
were dead cattle, our breath

wet hide. They could flush us
by our reek. We
hanged informants. They
shot prisoners. Every one

of us died. Everyone
lay open like eyes.

That night, a cloudburst scraped our stench
like scales off the bloody grass.

And a Great Part of Me Will Escape the Grave
—near Dahlonega, Georgia

Yellow as the late October sun
there was a dust in these hills

once, and other peoples,
long departed. Might as well

honor the bumblebees, felling-
saw loud. Might as well

mourn grass. What was carved
has given up its hold:

blank as quicksilver
these Hickory Flats gravestones,

slate weathered smooth
by scarcity and years. All

had a name, a first day,
a last one as themselves.

No more. Still, someone
has brought flowers

paper-white and red:
plastic, two per grave.

Ask Me Something Else Original

Think the visage
a black-eyed Susan

shows a bee,
the body heat

a mouse can't keep
from a rattlesnake:

ourselves
to ourselves.

A child blind before birth
won't know a sunset's

every trick, a sighted child
all that night can't steal.

What we might grasp
keeps us incomplete.

What we can't miss
makes us whole.

Then Let Yourself Love All That

So much only can we ask
      of gods, and what we
may shape out of a cloud is not
      that cloud: another to hold,
children to live to be
      let go. Death isn't the storm
we face: to be not the god

we can dream of
but the god we ourselves
can be—you forgive me, here's more time.
      Let's hold on however long
we have and praise. Not that
      we lack, but that we can do
so much lacking.

Street's End

Consider, once more,
the universal cannibalism of the sea.

But nothing does, of course:
the avocado sofa in the weeds

will keep some time, a whaling ship
of corduroy and springs,

sea-struck, side-split, gutted
on a beach of motor oil and gravel,

the world itself now sunk
rammed by a monster storm,

its few survivors mustering
what dignity catastrophe can spare—

the arms of laundry posts
barnacled with rust

but open still, the calcinated box
of a pine dresser, gray with age

but still willing to hold
the secrets of earthworms.

A skeletal Ford.
Its vaguely human form.

Petrichor

Ripples on the pond are the pond
in flow, clouds old water

once a turkey or a black
vulture: roadkill, beak, vulture.

We and these mayflies to this oak,
to all this petrichor

Underworld

for my father

A pale heron flew over swamp water,
its shadow on shadows. We both saw it.

You were alone but didn't yet know.
What don't cypresses know

that they must? Some blessed trees.
We are nothing but others.

Looking for Migrants
also for my father

Him: a brackish lagoon,
the sun a wire hyssop
on my lips. He never walked

this salt-coarse sand
my blistered feet
trace their search on.

      * * *

The only thirst here:
mine. Sanderlings and dunlins

drink the Atlantic, snort
its brine, will soon breed summer

again in Hudson Bay.
Unless I come too close

I am not
of their world.

      * * *

Like the least terns,
he came north to Florida
bruised in the crossing:

everything that flies
takes off and lands
into the wind,

that *spiritus mundi*—
aloft, who knows
what furies await.

* * *

A rare bird on this beach:
a rufous fowl, adrift

with the tide. He did not fly
nor try to fly. I gave him

one dry night
on a full stomach,

carried him
light as ashes in another box.

He had no name I knew.
He did not live

in any guidebook.
I've watched

for others since, intuiting
birds weren't migrants once

but grew into it, that balance
of need: to settle in lack

or to go on looking
for what isn't there.

Endgame

My sea of change
is reefed with wrecks:

for *wreck*, read
out of choices,

for *choices*, read
time. Sometimes

a ship finds shore:
for *shore*, read

another door closing,
door meaning

a storm,
wailing still.

Acknowledgements

My gratitude to the following journals where earlier versions of these poems first appeared:

AGNI: "Blucher, Arendt, A Wildland Fire" and "From the Lost Letters to Matias Perez, Aeronaut"
A-Minor: "Trail Mountain" and "Looking for Migrants"
The Banyan Review: "Dead People's Things for Sale," "Mayport Ospreys," and "Using the Scout's Handbook While Learning English"
Barrow Street: "We Argued in Spanish Before We Argued in English"
Burning House Press: "Confession"
The Collapsar: "December Doe" and "Underworld"
Diode Poetry Journal: "In the Dark Times" and "St. Augustine in Ariel's Island"
First Things: "The Prodigal's Next Life"
Madcap Review: "Jesus Drowns in the Sea of Galilee" and "Rifle Grease, Gun Powder, Dead Fish"
Massachusetts Review: "October"
New England Review : "Virgilian Fortunes," "Watercolors at Year's End," "Summertime," "What Vallejo Calls Notre Dame Bridge," and "Street's End"
Poetry Northwest: "Learning to See in Another Language"
Potluck: "Kahina"
Psaltery and Lyre: "I Am Prometheus"
riverSedge: "After Finishing This Poem"
Scalawag: "And a Great Part of Me Will Escape the Grave"
The Shore: "Third Winter in Our Second Country," "Soon Before All Light Is Gone"
Wombwell Rainbow: "Petrichor"

About the Author

Andres Rojas is the author of the chapbook *Looking for What Isn't There* (Paper Nautilus Press Debut Series Winner, 2019) and the audio-only chapbook *The Season of the Dead* (EAT Poems, 2016). His poetry has been featured in the *Best New Poets* series and has appeared in, among others, *AGNI, Barrow Street, Colorado Review, Massachusetts Review, New England Review,* and *Poetry Northwest.*

About the Artist

Born in Ecuador, Francisco Alvarado's journey as an artist began when he was six years old. In the early 1980s, Francisco's interest in technology, especially the introduction of the Apple computer, gave him a new tool to create art and he learned to code. This decision helped him developed a career working for the entertainment industry. Every experience for Francisco has been used to augment and broaden his visual communication. Combining his experiences, traditional paintings, and technology, Francisco continues to create and show his work both in Los Angeles and on social networks.

ABOUT THE BOOK

Third Winter in Our Second Country was designed at Trio House Press
through the collaboration of:

Tayve Neese, Lead Editor
Sarah Dumitrascu, Supporting Editor
Joel Coggins, Cover Design
Matt Mauch, Interior Design

The text is set in Adobe Caslon Pro.

The publication of this book is made possible, whole or in part,
by the generous support of the following individuals or agencies:

Anonymous

ABOUT THE PRESS

Trio House Press is an independent literary press publishing three or more collections of poems annually. Our Mission is to promote poetry as a literary art enhancing culture and the human experience. We offer two annual poetry awards: the Trio Award for First or Second Book for emerging poets and the Louise Bogan Award for Artistic Merit and Excellence for a book of poems contributing in an innovative and distinct way to poetry. We also offer an annual open reading period for manuscript publication.

Trio House Press adheres to and supports all ethical standards and guidelines outlined by the CLMP.

Trio House Press, Inc. is dedicated to the promotion of poetry as literary art, which enhances the human experience and its culture. We contribute in an innovative and distinct way to poetry by publishing emerging and established poets, providing educational materials, and fostering the artistic process of writing poetry. For further information, or to consider making a donation to Trio House Press, please visit us online at www.triohousepress.org.

Other Trio House Press books you might enjoy:

The Traditional Feel of the Ballroom by Hannah Rebecca Gamble / 2021

Sweet Beast by Gabriella R. Tallmadge / 2021 Louise Bogan Award Winner selected by Sandy Longhorn

Songbox by Kirk Wilson / 2020 Trio Award Winner selected by Malena Mörling

YOU DO NOT HAVE TO BE GOOD by Madeleine Barnes / 2020

X-Rays and Other Landscapes by Kyle McCord / 2019

Threed, This Road Not Damascus by Tamara J. Madison / 2019

My Afmerica by Artress Bethany White / 2018 Trio Award Winner selected by Sun Yung Shin

Waiting for the Wreck to Burn by Michele Battiste / 2018 Louise Bogan Award Winner selected by Jeff Friedman

Cleave by Pamel Johnson Parker / 2018 Trio Award Winner selected by Jennifer Barber

Two Towns Over by Darren C. Demaree / 2018 Louise Bogan Award Winner selected by Campbell McGrath

Bird~Brain by Matt Mauch / 2017

Dark Tussock Moth by Mary Cisper / 2016 Trio Award Winner selcted by Bhisham Bherwani

The Short Drive Home by Joe Osterhaus / 2016 Louise Bogan Award Winner selected by Chard DeNiord

Break the Habit by Tara Betts / 2016

Bone Music by Stephen Cramer / 2015 Louise Bogan Award Winner selected by Kimiko Hahn

Rigging a Chevy into a Time Machine and Other Ways to Escape a Plague by Carolyn Hembree / 2015 Trio Award Winner selected by Neil Shepard

Magpies in the Valley of Oleanders by Kyle McCord / 2015

Your Immaculate Heart by Annmarie O'Connell / 2015

The Alchemy of My Mortal Form by Sandy Longhorn / 2014 Louise Bogan Award Winner selected by Peter Campion

What the Night Numbered by Bradford Tice / 2014 Trio Award Winner selected by Carol Frost

Flight of August by Lawrence Eby / 2013 Louise Bogan Award Winner selected by Joan Houlihan

The Consolations by John W. Evans / 2013 Trio Award Winner selected by Mihaela Moscaliuc

Fellow Odd Fellow by Stephen Riel / 2013

Clay by David Groff / 2012 Louise Bogan Award Winner selected by Michael Waters

Gold Passage by Iris Jamahl Dunkle / 2012 Trio Award Winner selected by Ross Gay

If You're Lucky Is a Theory of Mine by Matt Mauch / 2012

CPSIA information can be obtained
at www.ICGtesting.com
Printed in the USA
LVHW090851150721
692729LV00002B/107